INTRODUCTION

Although there are about 4,500 mammalian species on earth, only a very select few enjoy high popularity as household pets. One group of these are the gerbils and jirds. In particular, the Mongolian jird, or gerbil as it is more commonly known, has established

use___ _____ _____ __ _____ ____ers. It was found to be a hardy, easy to keep little creature. As it became more readily bred and domesticated under laboratory conditions, a number found their way into the pet market. This happened during the 1950s. From

There are about 80 species of gerbils in the wild. Their range of distribution extends from China and Mongolia through Asia and into Africa.

itself as a frontrunner in the 'most popular pets' category. Of the rodents that are kept as pets, only the hamster and the ubiquitous mouse are seen in greater numbers.

The gerbil, rather like the hamster before it, owes its pet popularity to the fact that it became a well liked small rodent

those individuals, a whole hobby has developed around the gerbil.

As pet gerbil numbers increased, color mutations started to appear. These always attract extra attention. The gerbil is now seen in a wide range of colors and patterns. For the serious enthusiast, there are gerbil clubs, and you can exhibit quality stock just as you can a dog, cat, rabbit or hamster.

As a small cage pet, the gerbil makes a fine choice. It has the needed attributes of being clean, inoffensive, easy to accommodate, low-cost to purchase, and readily bred if this aspect appeals to you. Although related to mice, its longer rear legs and tufted tail often make it more acceptable to

Meriones unguiculatus, this being the species you will likely see in your pet store. Its natural distribution range is Mongolia, southern Siberia, Manchuria and northern China.

Like all gerbils it lives in a burrow system. The complexity of this will reflect the size of the family unit. The burrow extends downwards, at an angle, to a

Gerbils come in a wide variety of colors, with new colors certain to appear in the future.

the moms of the world. Unlike the hamster, most gerbils will cohabit with their own kind without undue fighting—another plus.

GERBILS IN THE WILD

The habits of the various gerbil species in the wild differ according to the species. For our purposes we will focus on

depth of about 1-2 feet. Its length is usually only a few feet before it rises back to the surface. Other species may have very similar homes, or lengthy and complex burrows.

Within the burrow there will be one or more nesting chambers, as well as food stores and a latrine area. Mongolian gerbils are social,

Since its introduction to the pet-keeping public in the 1960s, the gerbil has continued to grow in popularity in the world of small-mammal pets.

living in family units comprising a male, female and their immature offspring. They are both nocturnal and diurnal, meaning they are active both during the night and day. While being social within family units, this does not apply to strangers who will be attacked if they attempt to enter a family unit.

This species exhibits a better than average gerbil ability to tolerate a range of temperatures and humidity. It may forage on the surface in subzero temperatures, as well as when these are over 38°C (100°F) during hot summers. It neither hibernates nor estivates (short periods of torpidity). Under very adverse conditions it may, however, remain in its burrow for extended periods. It dines on its stored food.

The diet comprises fruits, vegetables and quite a lot of grain/seeds. It will eat invertebrates (worms, insects and their like) and will not be averse to some carrion, or the newly born offspring of other small rodents that it may encounter during its foraging trips. The typical home range in the Mongolian species may extend over a kilometer, quite a distance for such a little critter: this is a very active animal.

In the wild the gerbil has many enemies. These range from mammals, such as foxes and stoats, to birds of prey and reptilians, especially snakes. Its defensive strategy is either to outrun them with its leaping progression, dive into its burrow, remain immobilized and hope it will go unnoticed, or hide in any available crevice.

Gerbils have been subject to poisoning campaigns when their activities have clashed with human habitation. In some ways, however, proximity to human settlement has aided them because many of the gerbil's predators are also persecuted by humans. Furthermore, agriculture does provide these little rodents with a ready source of food.

In this book, we will discuss all relevant aspects of maintaining these charming little pets within a domestic environment. Additionally, in the final chapter, the more exotic species are discussed. These have become more popular in recent years, a trend likely to continue.

Gerbils are very social little animals and should not be kept singly. They do best when kept in pairs or small groups.

One of the first color mutations to appear in gerbils was the albino. Albinos are all white and have red eyes.

bred in much larger numbers than gerbils, which explains the larger number of color forms. Mutations tend to appear in ratio to the population as a whole.

The following are the present color forms you can select from in gerbils. Their genetic base, where known, is given in the table at the end of the chapter for those with an understanding of the subject.

Black: The genetic term for this color is non agouti. The mutation was first discovered in a Texas aerospace center about 1978. It results in extra deposits of melanin pigment. A good solid black is a very desirable gerbil for exhibition. Most examples will have some white hairs in the coat, and may tend to display a brown suffusion.

Albino: At the other extreme to black is albino. In this variety, the mutation prevents the formation of pigment. The result is an all white individual with pink eyes (this being the hemoglobin of the blood). Some yellow suffusion may be seen. This is often the result of abdominal skin secretions used for scent marking. Also, urine and bedding may stain the coat of this, and any other light colored

An agouti gerbil and a chinchilla, or gray agouti, gerbil. To many gerbil fanciers, breeding for new color varieties is the most exciting part of the hobby.

variety. What you should understand about albinos is they are not devoid of color pigment. Pigmentation is present, but unable to form. If an albino is mated with any color form all of the offspring will be colored and all will be carrying the albino gene. They are know as 'splits', meaning they carry the mutational gene but it is unable to express itself in that particular individual.

Pink-Eyed White or Dark-Tailed Variety: This mutation appeared in the late 1960s. It is an incomplete albino that sports some dark hairs on its tail. These are not evident until the age of about two or more months. The color is thermo sensitive. This means the dark hairs become lighter as the temperature increases, and vice versa. It could also be described an incomplete Himalayan. This is the pattern seen in cats (also known as Siamese), rabbits, and other pets where the points (face, feet and tail) are darker than the rest of the fur.

Gray Agouti or Chinchilla: In this variety the mutation suppresses the formation of yellow-red in the agouti hair. The

The black gerbil is one of the newer colors to become available commercially. A good specimen will be solid black throughout—with no stray white hairs or signs of fading color.

result is a gray color which could also be called a chinchilla, as in rabbits.

Argente: This color is variably called cinnamon, golden, or white bellied golden. It is a light sandy shade with a white underbelly. There should be a clear line of demarcation between these. The mutation dilutes or suppresses black pigmentation. Apart from affecting the coat, it makes the eye a pink to dark red. It is a very appealing color pattern.

Blue: You might be a little disappointed with this color. It is more of a gray than a blue. It was created by crossing the chinchilla color with black. This results in the black pigment being diluted in the hair cells.

Lilac: This form was the result of crossings using black and argente individuals. The argente gene dilutes the black to produce a light-medium gray. The eyes are ruby red.

Dove: This was created by pairing the lilac to the pink-eyed white. It is a paler version of the lilac. The two forms do have an overlap range making it difficult to establish which is which (genetically) without knowing the pairing that produced them.

Cream: This color was created by combining the argente with the pink-eyed white. The result is a very light golden. The eyes are pink.

White Patterned Forms: In most popular pets, such as rabbits, and hamsters, it is not long before white spotted or patched variants start to appear. These may be given various names according to the extent of white. Possibly the most well known examples of the 'spotting' genes are seen in piebald, Dutch pattern, and banded. The common thread with white spot genes is that they are very unpredictable in the way they express themselves. For example, one individual may be nearly all white with just a few dark marks (spots or patches). At the other end of the range, is the almost black individual with just a few white spots or patches. Two well marked individuals can mate to produce offspring that are poorly marked.

In contrast, two poorly marked examples can produce very nicely marked offspring. The white spot gene is, therefore, a very frustrating mutation to work with. But it is both challenging and fascinating in what it can produce. It is hoped a good Dutch pattern, as in rabbits and mice, will one day result from this mutation. Presently, it creates an unlimited range of bicolor patterned individuals, some of which are extremely attractive.

Other Colors & Patterns: As the numbers of gerbils increases, the potential for new mutations does likewise. These, together with their permutations with existing color patterns, will produce even more varieties. Amongst these will be chocolate, various shades of red, and numerous yellow and cream forms. Dappled or roan patterns are very likely, though they are often accompanied with

Argente gerbil. This attractive variety goes by a number of names, including cinnamon, golden, or white-bellied golden. Eye color can range from pink to dark red.

problems if planned breeding is not undertaken.

It is also probable that mutations affecting the coat, as seen in most other popular pets, will appear. These will include longhair, rex (curly), and satin. These new mutations can happen at any time. They may appear in the stock of an expert breeder, or that of a pet owner producing his first litter.

Possible Genotype of Some Gerbil Varieties

The table includes possible genotypes of varieties not yet available. These may be useful as a guide to breeders when they do appear. The genetic status of some existing color forms has not been fully established. This is why certain of these in the table appear the same.

AGOUTI	AA	Brown	aabb
NON AGOUTI (BLACK)	aa	Pink-Eyed White	pp
BLUE	aadd or aapp	White Spot (bicolor)	SpSp or Spsp
GRAY OR CHINCHILLA	AApp	Lilac	aadd
HIMALAYAN	$c^h c^h$	Dove	aaddpp
CREAM	aabbpp or aaee	Argente	aabb or AApp
LONGHAIR	ll	Rex	rere
SATIN	SaSa or Sasa		

Dove gerbil. This variety is actually a paler version of the lilac.

There are also color varieties with various white markings.
This is an agouti Canadian white spot gerbil.

HOUSING

Gerbils and similar small rodents are very easy to cater for in respect of housing needs. You have three options: 1) An aquarium, 2) Any of the cages now manufactured for small mammals, and 3) One of the numerous habitat tube systems.

units are deemed less desirable, though many people use them.

The advantage of a larger unit is it provides much greater scope for being furnished in an interesting manner for the residents. It gives them excellent exercise facility, and looks

An aquarium is an excellent choice for gerbil housing. It can be easily cleaned and furnished and provides optimum viewing pleasure for the gerbil owner.

AQUARIUMS

The plexiglass aquarium has the advantage of being easy to clean, transparent, available in a number of sizes to suit your finances, and easily furnished. An ideal size would be 24x18x12in (60x45x30cm) which approximates a 22 US gal (19 UK gal) tank. Larger units are usually regarded as better, while smaller

esthetically pleasing. The aquarium will need either a hood, or a weld wire mesh cover, to remove the possibility the gerbil might jump out of its home.

SMALL MAMMAL CAGES

Manufactured cages for gerbils, hamsters, mice and their like come in a very extensive range of sizes and options. Always try to

Pet shops stock toys and other cage accessories for gerbils.

obtain the largest your budget will permit. Do check with a number of pet stores to see the models they stock. Some will come complete with nest box and raised platform, maybe even including an exercise wheel. Others are very basic and the furnishings must be purchased as extras. In some models, the metal top detaches from a plastic base for ease of cleaning. Others are made using sheet metal for the base. The problem with these is they eventually become rusted from urine making cleaning more difficult. You should check there are no sharp projections on the inner cage bars which could injure your pet. Usually, the more costly the cage the better its quality of construction, and the longer its wear life will be.

HABITAT SYSTEMS

Originally designed for hamsters, the habitat systems represent a real attempt to reproduce a wild rodent's home. There is a basic kit comprising a plastic tub with one or more tubes connecting this to another tub. You can add more tubes, and tubs, to create a very elaborate labyrinth comprising feed, toilet, nesting, and exercise areas. The negatives of the systems, compared to the other options, are their cost, greater difficulty in cleaning, and in accessing them to lift out your pets. But they are innovative.

FURNISHING THE GERBIL'S HOUSE

The following items range from the necessary to those which will add interest for the gerbil, and for you as an observer.

Floor Covering: The most popular covering will be sawdust or wood shavings. Sawdust is very absorbent, a beneficial feature, but can irritate the eyes, ano-genital region, and will cling to moist foods. It may also cause irritation to the nostrils, and create problems if swallowed.

Avoid sawdust from cedar. The phenols in it are very dangerous to small mammals. White pine is better, and hardwoods more safe, but rather less absorbent. Pine or hardwood shavings are less likely to create problems, but are less absorbent.

Better than sawdust, or wood shavings, are the numerous wood fiber and pulp bedding materials now commercially produced. They are biodegradable, odor absorbing, last longer, and are sanitized to kill bacteria, mold and fungus. However, they are much more expensive.

Other potential coverings are shredded, granulated, or sheet paper, and corncobs. Additionally, natural commercial fiber bedding can be used as bedding material for rodents. Hay can be used, but has the disadvantage that it may contain fungal or bacterial spores, or the eggs of parasites. Wood wool, as used in packing cases, should not be used. It can become entangled around the feet or neck of pets—especially youngsters.

Avoid sand as a general floor covering—it is abrasive. Garden soil, which may contain many pathogens (disease causing organisms), is another substance

A gravity-fed water bottle, which can be easily attached to the side of the cage, is a good means of providing water.

best avoided unless it has been baked in an oven. The floor covering layer should be generous. In a large unit you could make a little area that mimics the gerbil's natural terrain. This could contain a little sand mixed with small aquarium gravels, and maybe a little quality potting soil.

heavy, so it is not easily tipped over, and is easily cleaned. Water can be supplied via a similar container, or via a hamster water bottle. In the latter case, buy the best. This will not leak as might the cheaper models. Be sure it is placed where the gerbil can reach it easily. In an aquarium, you will have to suspend it on wire.

Housing made of wood is not recommended for gerbils, as they will gnaw on it to keep their teeth worn down. Additionally, the animals' urine can eventually cause the wood to rot.

Nestbox: Your gerbil must have a nestbox in which to retreat and sleep. It should have a small entrance, and be large enough inside to cater for the number of pets you have in the housing.

Nestboxes can be purchased from pet stores, or are easily fashioned from small plastic tubs.

Food/Water Containers: The recommended food receptacle is an earthenware (crock) pot. It is

Check that the spout of the bottle does not touch anything (such as floor covering), otherwise it will tend to leak and make the floor very wet.

Exercise Wheel: These are always advised for caged animals. Your pet will spend quite some time in this, keeping fit as a result. There are many models to choose from, this author preferring the solid tread type.

Four-week-old youngster. Play helps to reduce stress and makes for a more relaxed pet.

SELECTING A GERBIL

The way in which you go about selecting your first gerbil(s) should reflect your objective. If you are looking for a pet your prime concerns should be that it is young, healthy and of a color that appeals to you. Your local pet store should be able to satisfy your needs. If you plan to become a serious breeder you will also want them to be of good quality in respect to their conformation, color pattern, and ancestry. A few minor faults in a pet will not detract from their making good pets, but would be undesirable in breeding or exhibition stock.

Furthermore, the potential breeder may be better obtaining young adults rather than youngsters. Breeding and show stock are better obtained from a specialist breeder of the color you want, assuming color is of importance to you.

It is always wise to purchase your gerbil's accommodation

Young children should be supervised when they play with their gerbil pals.

before you obtain the pets. This way you can take your time seeking just the right housing. Then concentrate on obtaining really nice gerbils of the color and age you want. Most owners buy pets on an impulse; this is definitely the least desirable way to obtain any sort of pet.

ASSESSING HEALTH

Before inspecting any potential pet take a good look at the conditions under which the animals are living. If these are crowded, with dirty cages, and a lack of food and water, take your business to another supplier. This is the best way to register your disapproval of uncaring sellers.

Assuming the living conditions are good, the following are the key points to look for when assessing health:

Coat: This should be smooth and sleek. There should be no bald areas, no indication of flaky encrustations, or signs of parasitic infestation. Fleas and mites are uncommon in healthy domestic bred rodents. If present, they can be seen by brushing the coat against its lie, and by the presence of clusters of red or black specks. These are the fecal droppings of these parasites. They indicate unclean conditions.

Skin: This should be free of any swellings, cuts, or abrasions. Swellings, in particular, are not a healthy sign because they may be tumors.

Teeth: Try to inspect the teeth to see they are correctly aligned. This is very important for any rodent. The upper incisor teeth should be situated just over, but touching, those of the lower jaw. Any indication of non alignment should not be acceptable to you. If the teeth are not aligned correctly they will continue to grow up or down as the case may be. Besides making feeding difficult to impossible, they might pierce, or curl outside of the jaw.

General Observations: The eyes should be round and clear, with no signs of weeping. The nostrils should display no indication of a liquid discharge,

nor be swollen. The ears should be short, erect and non wrinkled. The tail should be straight, with no kinks in it. The feet should all have clawed digits. The anal region should be clean, with no signs of either staining from diarrhea, or hardened fecal matter clinging to it. Inspect the front feet. These must not be wet—which would indicate the animal has been wiping its nose with its feet—a very unhealthy sign.

A small carrying cage such as this is ideal for transporting your gerbil. Note the well-ventilated roof.

Watch the gerbil move around to ascertain that it displays no limp or difficulty in moving. If so, this might only be a temporary muscle injury, but could also indicate a hereditary problem.

Finally, cast an eye over all the other stock to see whether any others look unwell—especially those in the same cage as your potential pet. If there is, it is quite possible your choice may be infected but the problem is not yet manifest. This might happen within days of your taking it home. The gerbil, even a high quality example, is not an expensive pet. There is no reason to accept any but the fittest of individuals.

CHOICE OF SEX

If you are seeking a single pet its sex is not important, both are excellent. The male will have a somewhat stronger odor due to its scent secretions, but this is not excessive. If you want to keep two gerbils together females are less quarrelsome. Two males will share a habitat, but with greater risk of fighting, especially if they can scent females kept in other cages. Do not keep males and females together unless you want to be presented with litter after litter of babies.

BEST BUYING AGE

Young gerbils are weaned at about three weeks of age. A good buying age is therefore when they are four or more weeks old. By this time, they should be eating independently without problem. A youngster is the best choice for a pet. It will tame rapidly and you will have more years of enjoyment than if it is already an adult.

If you plan to be a breeder, a mature juvenile (four or more months old) would be a better choice. Its quality, both in its physique and color, will be more apparent. If you plan to commence with a trio you are advised to start with at least a proven male and two young females, or a trio of proven breeders. You might commence with stock that has already won some awards in exhibition, or has been bred from top winning parents.

SELECTING QUALITY

The only way you can appraise quality in gerbils is by seeing many examples—preferably those of show quality. Visit small mammal exhibitions where gerbils

It is a good idea to select a young gerbil. A young gerbil is easier to tame and will likely become friendlier than one that is purchased when it is already an adult.

If you do not plan to breed your gerbils, purchase only females. They will live together more peaceably than will males of the species.

are being shown. The same comment applies to color and pattern. Where solid colors are desired, such as black, argente, blue, dove and others, these should be as even as possible, not patchy or containing other colored hairs in the coat. Be prepared to pay much more for well bred examples, and even more if they display excellent color, or are of the newer color varieties. The exotic species of gerbils discussed in the final chapter will be more expensive than the popular pet that is the subject of this book.

KEEPING GERBILS WITH OTHER RODENTS

You are not recommended to keep gerbils in the same housing with other small rodents, such as hamsters or mice. Hamsters are belligerent little creatures who prefer their own company. They could inflict serious damage on a gerbil. Mice, like gerbils, are more sociable, but are still best kept with their own kind.

Even when you have a number of gerbils in the same accommodation it is not wise to introduce a stranger. It will probably be harassed, and may even be killed by the resident pets. If you want to have two or more gerbils in the same housing, it's best to buy these together as youngsters.

ARE GERBILS LEGAL IN YOUR AREA?

The final advice with respect to purchasing a gerbil is to find out if they can legally be kept as a pet in your state or area. In most states of the USA, Canada, and other countries, they are legal pets, but not always. In the USA, even if they are legal within the state, there may be local ordinances prohibiting them as pets.

Pet owners often wonder why this should be so. The answer is that some state wildlife departments are concerned that gerbils and other comparable pets may escape and establish themselves in the wild. They may disrupt the delicate ecological balance of nature where other indigenous animals are concerned. They might also prove to be pests where grain crops are grown. You can check with your local USDA office, or the Department of Fish and Wildlife. Your pet shop may know if there are any local restrictions.

It is true that many illegal pets are kept by owners. You are cautioned that apart from confiscation of the pets the fines can be heavy for breaking pet keeping laws.

This 17-day-old gerbil is already hand tame. When holding a gerbil, cup it securely in your hands but do not squeeze it. Remember that temperament can vary: some gerbils may be more amenable to handling than will others.

HANDLING

The correct way to lift a gerbil, if it's not friendly enough to be scooped in the hand, is as follows. Usher it into a corner of its cage and grasp the base of its tail —- never the tip. Lift gently, while placing your hand under the body to provide support. Be sure to teach young children this method. If they grasp and dangle the pet by the tip of its tail this will be painful and fearful to the gerbil. In this state it may either wriggle and be dropped to the floor, with risk of injury, or it may turn and bite the finger of the child. It will also be less inclined to be handled in the future.

Toys with holes in them should be appropriately sized for your pet.

GERBIL NUTRITION

Like most rodents, gerbils are very easy to cater for in respect of their nutritional needs. They are primarily herbivorous, meaning their diet is seeds, fruits and vegetables. But they will eat some animal protein foods, depending on their individual appetites. In the wild this would include varied insects and other invertebrates. The diet of your pet should comprise commercial preparations sold for hamsters, mice or rats, plus a range of fresh (high moisture content) foods, most of which are found in home kitchens. To these can be added various other items that will be beneficial, and relished by your pets. It will not cost a lot to keep one or more gerbils. Before discussing specific food items let us look at a few aspects related to nutrition.

MISCELLANEOUS ASPECTS OF FEEDING

Balance: Each food item contains a given number of constituents that are held in variable ratios, one to the other, in different foods. The key to successful nutrition is to provide these constituents in a balanced form so none are missing from the diet—nor are they being given in excess of metabolic needs. What a pet should eat and what it will eat are not always the same. You must balance the diet so the pet is not allowed to gorge on favored items at the expense of needed items. The best way to achieve this is to provide a variety of foods so the gerbil does not become finicky because its diet is limited to a few items.

When to Feed: Your gerbil should always have access to dry foods, such as seeds, on a free choice basis. Moist foods are best supplied in the evening. They will stay fresher overnight in a non temperature controlled home. Gerbils are generally more active at this time.

How Much to Feed: Given that dry foods are fed on a free choice basis, the quantity of food supplied is related to the fresh (moist) foods. This should be the amount consumed during a few hours period. Commence with a small amount. If this is all eaten rapidly you can increase the quantity a little at a time at subsequent meals until you establish the pet's typical appetite. When most animals are given generous access to foods, coupled with adequate space and exercise facility, they will normally eat only what they need to remain in a fit condition. However, in cramped quarters, and when bored or stressed, they can develop eating and drinking syndromes that result in obesity.

If this happens, the answer is to address the underlying problem while reducing the amount of food a little at a time.

The range of foods should remain the same. You might also reduce the quantity of any seeds and nuts containing a high protein or fat content. Never feed foods of vegetable origin in a sudden glut. This can result in scouring, a condition characterized by diarrhea. Softfoods should be introduced on a build-up basis. Always rinse fruits and foods. If you observe a gerbil not eating as much as normal, or is slower than normal coming to take favored items, these may be early signs of a health problem. You can watch the individual carefully over the next twenty-four hours, removing it if the appetite reduces, or if physical signs of a problem become apparent.

Oodles, manufactured by the Nylabone® Corporation, will satisfy your gerbil's urge to gnaw. They are available in several flavors.

vegetables to remove residual chemicals that may be on them from crop spraying.

Observe Your Gerbils: It is very important you always observe the feeding habits of your gerbils—especially if a number share the same accommodation. You will be aware of their individual appetites, and of any preferences each has for certain

Factors Influencing Appetite: All animals will display a curve in their appetite. Many factors will influence total food intake.

Exercise: A very active pet will eat in relation to its level of activity.

Age: Young gerbils will eat progressively more food until they reach maturity (4-6 months of age). Intake will then fall back somewhat depending on the amount of physical activity it undertakes and the other factors discussed here. An old gerbil will eat less than when it was in its prime.

Temperature: If the environmental temperature drops for any period of time this will tend to increase the appetite. Extra food is needed for conversion to energy used in keeping warm.

Reproductive State: A breeding female's food intake will rise as she nears birthing a litter, and in the immediate weeks that follow.

Health State: An ailing gerbil's appetite will normally fall. As it recovers it will need extra quality foods to replace the muscle tissues converted to energy while it was ill.

Mental State: A stressed pet may eat more or less food, depending on how the stress affects the individual.

Rodents need hard things on which to gnaw. If these are not supplied in the form of hard biscuit, baked bread, tree branches, and wooden playthings, their teeth may become too long. When this happens they will not be able to eat as normal. Your vet can trim the teeth, after which you must correct the diet.

Should you be confronted with an appetite problem in your pet, do consider each of these factors when trying to determine the problem.

FOOD TYPES

Food can be divided into two basic types based on (1) nutrient composition, and use value in the body and (2) actual form, be this dry or moist.

Nutrient Composition: All foods contain proteins, fats, carbohydrates, minerals and water in different ratios. Each of these compounds perform particular functions in the body. They are collectively required to ensure good health and growth. If the diet sways too much towards one group of ingredients (such as proteins or carbohydrates) health will suffer.

Proteins provide the building blocks of muscle and other tissues (brain, blood, genes). They are especially important in young growing gerbils, breeding females, and those recovering from illness. Carbohydrates are energy foods used for day to day muscular activity. They should form the staple part of the diet. Fats give food its unique taste. They are used for insulating bone and muscle, and in helping transport other nutrients around the body via the blood.

Minerals are needed for cell structure, and for controlling the rate of osmosis between cells. This is the process that allows fluids to move between tissues at a regulated rate. When this does not happen as it should, problems will ensue.

Water is the most important 'food' because it accounts for the bulk of any animal's body weight. Without this precious liquid, in the needed volume, all metabolic processes suffer: they deteriorate in performance. The functions discussed are simplistic because each of the groups are part of a very complex series of inter-related chemical reactions.

Food Forms: All foods contain moisture to a greater or lesser degree. Seeds have little liquid content, fruits and vegetables are nearly all liquid. Your gerbil needs both, plus access to fresh water on a daily basis. It is true these

Gerbils in the wild will die before they reach their lifespan potential.

The advantage of dry foods is they provide nutrients in a concentrated form compared, on a weight basis, to moist foods.

Their shelf life is longer, as is their exposure life once fed to your pets. Moist foods quickly deteriorate as the temperature increases. They also attract

The commercial dry food mixes that are sold for hamsters, mice, or rats are suitable for a gerbil. Dry food should be supplied fresh daily.

animals are able to exist in arid areas where water is scarce. They carefully regulate their water loss (sweating, urine and fecal water content) to match their intake. Even so, under domestic conditions, by having access to water on a daily basis you ensure there is no risk they will suffer from dehydration. You want your pet to live a long and healthy life.

unwanted insects and microorganisms more readily than dry foods.

The advantage of moist (soft) foods is that many, such as fruits, contain high levels of vitamins. Moist foods are also more readily eaten and digested, important considerations in young, ailing or older individuals. Under the moist food heading are also included livefoods, such as invertebrates, and those of animal origin. These contain certain amino acids—the precursors of proteins—not found in vegetables.

FOOD PRESENTATION

Dry foods are normally supplied as a mixture in their own dish. You can also scatter some in the cage so your pet has to work a little to obtain its rations, much as it would in the wild. If this is done, it's essential the cage is kept very clean. The method is more wasteful than dish feeding, but is a stress reliever. Softfoods should be fed in a dish so they remain free of floor covering.

When new items are being considered, especially seeds, they can be fed in their own dish so you can assess their appeal to your pets. If initially ignored, you can add them to a mash of dry or moist foods in small quantities to give the gerbil the chance to become familiar with their taste.

Mashes containing a range of ingredients of plant and animal origins can be blended to make a weekly quantity that can be placed in the refrigerator and fed as needed. Be sure such foods are well thawed before feeding to your pets.

SOME POPULAR FOOD ITEMS

Although the pet owner will find it more convenient to purchase ready-mixed seeds, cereal crops, and rabbit pellets, the breeder may find it more economical, and beneficial, to prepare their own mixtures. The following gives the percentage of the dry weight or grams per 100 of the edible portion of major food groups. The percentages are given to underline the very considerable differences between food items, a fact not always appreciated.

HIGH PROTEIN FOODS:

Seeds: Linseed 21%, Sunflower, Rape 20%, Hemp 18%, Niger, Maw 17%, Canary 14%.

Nuts: Peanut 25g, Pistachio, Almond 19g, Cashew 17g, Walnut 15g, Hazelnut 13g, Pecan 9g, Chestnut 3.5g

Fruits & Vegetables: Generally low in proteins unless in dried form. Yeast (dried) 39g, Soybeans 34%, Lentils (dried) 25g Broad beans and Peas (dried) 24g, Kidney beans 23g, Potato (dried) 8g, Peas (unripe) 6g, Onions (dried) 5g, Apricots (dried) and Garlic 5g, Figs (dried 3.5g) Kale 4g, Apples & Peaches (dried 3g)

Meats & Poultry: The protein content is very variable based on the cut (rump, rib,) or part of the body, and whether the item is raw or cooked. The range can be from 9-23g. Fish generally have a good protein content.

HIGH FAT FOODS:

Any food item that has a high protein content will often have a goodly fat content. Exceptions are butter, cod-liver oil and most vegetable oils. These have a fat content ranging from 80-100%. Dairy products generally have high fat content.

HIGH CARBOHYDRATE FOODS:

Seeds: Wheat 74%, Millet 65%,

Maize 63%, Canary 58%

Fruits: Date (dried) 73g, Apricot 23g (dried 66g), Banana 22g, Persimmon 20g, Grape 17g, Currants (Black) 16g, Apple, Cherry, Pear 15g

Vegetables: Kidney beans 62g, Broad beans 58g, Garlic 29g, Potato (Sweet) 26g, Horseradish 18g, Parsnips, Peas 17g, o7 3 Beet 10g, Carrot, Dandelion 9g. Most vegetables have a low carbohydrate content unless dried, when it rises dramatically. Cereal crops and their byproducts (bread) have a high carbohydrate content, usually in the range of 50-80g.

An exercise wheel is a good addition to a gerbil's cage, but it should be of the kind that has an enclosed back. The open-rung type shown here can result in injury to the tail or claws.

VITAMIN FOODS:

As a general rule, all fruits, fish and vegetable oils, and animal livers have good vitamin content. This varies depending on the item and the vitamin. Supplying a range of items should ensure the needed amounts and balance are received. Be cautious when adding vitamin supplements to the diet of a pet already receiving a balanced diet. Excessive intake of some vitamins and minerals can be just as dangerous as a lack of them. Consult your vet if in doubt.

WILD PLANTS AND SEEDS

Your gerbil will enjoy eating many wild plants and seeds, and also the flowering heads of some plants. Care should be taken on two accounts. If you are unsure whether a given plant is poisonous do not feed it. Plants growing from bulbs are usually toxic to your pets, as are buttercups. Avoid gathering wild plants from areas that may have been treated with chemicals, fouled by vehicle exhaust fumes, or trampled by dogs and other livestock (road verges being the obvious areas).

Amongst the wild plants that can be fed are dandelion, chickweed, clover, coltsfoot, plantain, shepherd's purse and yarrow. Consult local plant guides for your area.

BREEDING AND EXHIBITION

Gerbils are very reliable breeders, so much so that unless you have a worthwhile objective there is little benefit in procreation for its own sake. This merely contributes to depressing the price of these pets, which are already low cost. It also lowers the standard of quality in the gerbil population as a whole.

Worthwhile objectives are: (1) to breed superior individuals that will make potential show exhibits (Those not reaching this standard will generally be better than if random breeding is practiced.) and (2) to try and develop better, or new, colors and patterns. (Color breeding is best left to the specialist until you develop a sound knowledge of how color is inherited.)

PRACTICAL AND COST CONSIDERATIONS

If you plan to breed you will require a number of extra cages in which to place the results of your breeding. Sexes must be kept separate once they reach breeding age. You will need to keep more food, and have more space available for your stock. This will all increase your hobby's overhead expenses. You should not assume the fees for selling stock will equate your cost of breeding. This is most unlikely for the average hobbyist.

Even on a small scale, the time you need to spend with your stock will increase considerably— don't forget all the extra cleaning chores. You should ask yourself the following:

a) Do I have the time, space and cash to conduct a breeding program?

b) What do I hope to achieve?

c) How will I sell the surplus offspring?

CONTROLLED BREEDING

If you decide to breed gerbils it's important you undertake a controlled program. This has two meanings. Firstly, always limit the number of breedings to your ability to sell the surplus offspring. If this is not done, you will quickly find things getting out of hand. You will be short of space, short of cages and equipment, and short of time. Your costs will rise disproportionately to your returns. This leads to frustration and disappointment. As a result, you will lose enthusiasm or your husbandry standards will fall. Many enthusiastic beginners leave animal hobbies essentially because their expectations were set too high and because they allowed their stock to breed in an uncontrolled manner.

The second meaning of 'controlled' is that you, rather than the gerbils, determine who is to mate with whom. If you simply place a male with a number of females and let nature take its

Gerbils can be sexed at about the age of four weeks. This is a male.

course, this is not true breeding in any worthwhile sense. You must plan each mating with care based on your expectations from it. The results should be recorded in breeding ledgers. A little at a time, the standard of your stock should get better. If this is not the reality, then the program is a failure. Always remember that quality stock costs no more to house and feed than does that which is mediocre. Nice gerbils will be easier to sell, and at better prices.

MAKING A START

Using the advice discussed, you should try to obtain the finest breeding stock you can. Do not assume your cherished pets are good enough to be worthy of breeding. Visit small mammal shows where gerbils are on view. You will see most, if not all, the available colors and patterns. Talk to breeders of the color you like best. Purchase exhibition quality stock — a trio (male and two females) makes a fine start. Breeding stock can be of various sorts. The most costly will be proven breeders that are young, and which have already enjoyed show success. Then there is quality proven stock that has not been exhibited, but is from a good breeder's line.

Older gerbils that are past their prime as exhibits, or even as prolific breeders, still have value to a beginner if they are paired to young unproven partners. They will still pass their genes to the smaller numbers of offspring the litter may contain. As a guide,

once a female is 15-18 months old she has reached her breeding peak.

The least costly stock will be unproven youngsters from a quality line. Examples of the rarer or more desirable colors will be more expensive than those which are readily available — but if these are what you really want, then the price is worth it.

BREEDING RECORDS

Do not attempt to keep breeding records in your head — it's not possible. You need written records. There are those records for individual gerbils, and those of actual breeding results.

Individual cards should indicate the gerbil's number, its age, sex, color, genotype (if known), parents (if known), breeder, and age at death. The logs may also record to which partners a particular has been mated, and the number of offspring produced. On the reverse side you might detail any other useful information— illnesses, treatments, or show wins.

Breeding cards should indicate the name or number of the paired gerbils, age at mating, date of mating, litter due, litter born, the number of offspring, sexes and colors. You might indicate which died before sale age, why (if known), as well as prices obtained for stock. The offspring retained should be given their individual records.

Other records can be maintained, such as medical, exhibition, and those used for grading stock. The most important thing is to maintain the records you commence. Keep them suited to your ability to do this.

PRACTICAL BREEDING

Having acquired your initial breeding stock, and made all other preparations, you are ready to commence breeding your stock if they are old enough. Sexual maturity is reached by the age of about eight weeks, so any time

while natural, is counter to most objectives. This means you must monitor each mating to ensure the partners are compatible. Once a mating has been undertaken, the male can be left with the female for a while, or he can be removed. If left with his partner until after the litter is born, he will share in the parental duties. However, a female may be mated *post partum*, meaning shortly after giving birth to a litter. The sperm will be stored in her body

A black gerbil and a silver gerbil mating. Gerbils may mate several times within a brief period.

after this will be fine. The first problem you are faced with is with respect to compatibility of the individuals.

In the wild, as discussed in the introduction, gerbils establish family units that do not tolerate intruders. Under controlled breeding you want litters only at your convenience. Establishing family units (colony breeding),

(delayed implantation). Once the current litter is weaned the next litter will begin development. You may not want this second litter, which is why the male must be removed prior to a litter being born.

When placing a pair of gerbils together, you must observe them carefully as fighting may follow. If this fighting is excessive you must intervene and separate the pair. Try again the following day to see if things are better.

Alternative methods are to place the pair in a 'honeymoon' cage, one which is neutral territory; this may prove better. You can also place a fine mesh divider screen between potential partners so they can familiarize themselves with each other's scent before they are actually introduced. Some fighting is normal with gerbil introductions, even with youngsters. However, it should never be allowed to reach the point where one partner is injured.

Once the pair settle down a mating will follow, but if the pair just do not get along, try them each with other partners. Most will be compatible given time to become familiar with each other. If you do decide to obtain youngsters, and allow them to remain as a family unit, you must be prepared for continual breeding. Your ability to be selective will largely be negated, other than at a group level.

The **estrus period** is the cycle during which a female is receptive to being mated — it is more commonly know as her 'heat'. It lasts about four days in gerbils and happens about every six days. These rodents, under domestic conditions, are potentially continual breeders, assuming conditions are favorable.

The **gestation period** is the time from fertilization of female eggs by the sperm until the time of giving birth (parturition). It is variable in gerbils within the range of 22-27 days, 25 being typical.

The litter size for a gerbil may vary with individual animals. A female may have as many as 10 babies, 4-7 being more likely. In theory, a female could have many litters per year, but this is not recommended if vigor and good health are prime considerations, which they should always be. Allow the female ample time between litters to rebuild her condition. Raising youngsters is physically draining on any female animal.

Gerbil babies are born blind, deaf and naked. They are fully furred within about a week. At this same time, their ears open and the eyes follow 3-5 days later. By the time the youngsters are about 16 days of age they will begin eating solid foods. They will be weaned when they are twenty-one days old. This can take a few days longer, so do not rush to place them in nursery cages unless you have seen them eating independent of their mother.

Once weaned, they can be transferred to a nursery cage for about a week. Thereafter, the sexes should be separated to avoid the possibility of early maturing individuals mating.

BREEDING PROBLEMS

A female having her first litter may panic. In this state, she may devour all or some of her first litter. Thereafter, she may be the perfect mother. If a female is not in sound breeding condition she may abort a litter or cannibalize it. She may also be cannibalistic if she is not receiving sufficient nutrition, is stressed in any way, or if the nestbox is infested with parasites, such as fleas or mites.

These possibilities aside, a female may simply be a poor mother and cannibalize or abandon her offspring. The problem could be genetic, in which case she should not be used for further breeding. It is also possible for poor motherhood to be inherited in a female via her

FOSTERING

If there is ever a need to foster offspring, it is best they are very young and of about the same age. Entice or wait for the female to leave the nest and place the fostered babies amongst the litter. To avoid the risk of rejection, because your scent is on the foster babies, you can wear surgical gloves, or use a plastic spoon to transfer them. Alternatively, if they are somewhat older, you can rub

Seventeen-day-old baby gerbils. A gerbil litter can be as large as ten, but four to seven is more the average.

father. However, genetic mothering problems are not common, and are difficult to establish with any certainty.

If the problems mentioned have been encountered, you are advised to consult your vet, the female may have an internal health problem. Generally, gerbils are very reliable breeders that experience few problems if they are well bred examples.

some soiled litter from the new mother's cage onto the babies.

Fostering can be useful if a mother dies, or if she has a large litter and another female has only one or two babies. You can mark the fostered infants with a water-based paint.

STOCK GRADING

When deciding which youngsters you want to retain for

future breeding the following are useful hints. You should purchase a more detailed book on selection methods. The book does not need be on gerbils, it could be on mice, rabbits or a general genetics book that covered grading methods. The principles are the same for all animals.

i) Your stock should be assessed by a good breeder or show judge. They can tell you the features you need to improve or concentrate on.

ii) Never get carried away by unimportant features. Your prime objects, in order of importance, should be health (including breeding vigor), temperament, conformation, and finally color/pattern.

iii) To fully assess stock you will need to keep them long enough to reach maturity. A youngster of 4-6 weeks can progress or regress by the time it is 16 weeks, or more, of age.

iv) You must be consistent in your evaluations—you must also be very aware what an excellent gerbil looks like.

v) You need to commit your gradings to paper if they are to have any long term value.

vi) You can assess individuals on the basis each must obtain a given minimum score for every feature, or a minimum score across all features. Never retain stock for the sake of doing so—if no individuals meet your predetermined standards, don't keep them.

EXHIBITION

Gerbil shows are one of the best ways you can perfect your hobby skills. You will learn from the experienced breeders in the hobby. Shows have many classes which you can enter. They will be for each sex, as well as for color and patterns. Your gerbils may need to be exhibited in special cages, or in any sort of cage, this depending on the country you live in and the regulations of the club organizing the show.

In general, mother gerbils are very attentive to their babies. These youngsters will be weaned when they are about 21 days of age.

Shows may be specifically for gerbils, but more often they will be part of a larger show in which other small rodents, such as mice or rats, are the main attraction. Contact a breeder in your locality to find out more about this very important area of the gerbil hobby.

An adult albino female. When selecting breeding stock, choose only those animals that are of sound temperament and in the best of health.

Argente male gerbil. In general, gerbils are hardy little animals. Good husbandry practices will go a long way in helping to maintain your pet's health.

HEALTH PROBLEMS

Gerbils are normally very hardy little mammals. However, under captive conditions they may succumb to any of the legion of problems and diseases that afflict other rodents and popular pets. In many instances the problems are avoidable, often stemming from a breakdown in sound husbandry techniques. If you appreciate that treating small mammals for a major illness can be difficult and costly, it becomes clear that preventative techniques have to be the best way to avoid illnesses. The thrust of this chapter will be based on this premise.

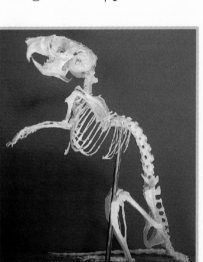

Skeleton of a gerbil. Note the length of the hind legs.

GENERAL HYGIENE

The easiest way for pathogens to gain access to your gerbil is via its housing. If this is not cleaned on a very regular basis, airborne bacteria will soon settle to form colonies that live on the food, fecal matter, and furnishing surfaces. Flies are carriers of all manner of diseases, and will also feed on fecal matter, and the pet's food — especially softfoods.

The cage must be thoroughly cleaned at least once every week.

Be sure to carefully wipe the cage bars. Pay extra attention to the corners of the cage. Feeding pots need cleaning daily. If they become chipped or cracked, replace them.

Breeding rooms should be planned with hygiene as a priority. Do not overcrowd a room with cages. The room should be light, airy, and well ventilated. Lack of ventilation is a major precursor of disease when numbers of animals are kept within a confined area.

All foods should be stored in suitable containers not exposed to flies, rodents, birds, or other potential vectors.

Soiled floor coverings must not be stored in waste bins in breeding rooms. Dispose of these as the cages are cleaned. Regulate the temperature to avoid rapid changes within twenty-four hour periods. These can badly stress gerbils and induce chills. From minor conditions, more serious illnesses may develop.

Humidity control to avoid high levels will be beneficial. Gerbils inhabit dry regions. Although the Mongolian species is able to adjust within certain limits, there is a secondary problem with high humidity levels. Bacteria and spores can be held within the moisture droplets to be released when the humidity level drops. Breeders should have some cages well away from their main stock into which any ill gerbils can be observed/ treated. — *See under Quarantine.*

Always wash your hands after handling any sick animal (gerbil or other pet). It is also prudent to be aware of any person who enters a breeding room who is a breeder of gerbils or other small mammals. Unless they maintain high standards of hygiene, they could transfer pathogens from their stock to yours via their clothing. You do not need to become paranoiac. But the more aware you are of how pathogens arrive in the breeding room, the better positioned you are to take all reasonable precautions to minimize this happening.

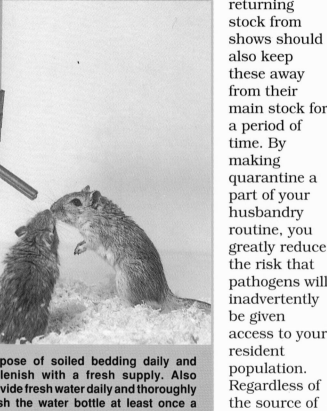

Dispose of soiled bedding daily and replenish with a fresh supply. Also provide fresh water daily and thoroughly wash the water bottle at least once a week.

QUARANTINE

Whether a breeder, or a pet owner with a number of established gerbils, you should never introduce additional stock to resident animals without subjecting them to a period of quarantine. The more gerbils you have, the more important this becomes. It is also recommended that exhibitors returning stock from shows should also keep these away from their main stock for a period of time. By making quarantine a part of your husbandry routine, you greatly reduce the risk that pathogens will inadvertently be given access to your resident population. Regardless of the source of new arrivals, and the fact that most of these — or individuals at a show — are healthy, there is always the chance this may not be so.

The quarantine period should be a minimum of fourteen days. This should be sufficient time for any incubating illness to manifest symptoms. During this period you can carefully monitor and adjust the feeding habits of the new arrivals to your regimen, and to your general environmental conditions, which will differ somewhat from those of the previous owner.

The multi-gerbil owner should also have a special treatment cage and isolation area for sick animals. A hospital cage should be maintained in scrupulous condition, being cleaned before and after each use. It should be placed in a location that is a few degrees warmer than that for the main stock. It needs no toys, just bare essentials such as nestbox, water and food pots.

Warmth alone can often correct minor chills and conditions. However, it must be well ventilated so that fresh air is circulated to remove airborne bacteria within the cage. Heat lamps are useful, but ensure they are sited outside, and at one end of, the cage. The animal must be able to move away from the heat if this starts to become uncomfortable. Monitor the temperature so that it does not exceed about 85°F (30°C), as this could induce heat stress. Ideal relative humidity will be 40-50%.

Gerbils groom themselves by using their tongue, teeth, and sometimes even their claws.

RECOGNIZING ILL HEALTH

You will easily be able to spot physical signs of an unhealthy gerbil. These will include diarrhea, running eyes or nose, dry flaky skin and fur, labored or noisy breathing, bald patches, lumps, abrasions or cuts. Indeed anything that is abnormal to what a healthy individual should look like is probably an indication of illness.

Unfortunately, some conditions and diseases may not display physical signs, or do so only when the problem has reached an advanced stage. In such cases, behavioral changes may be the only early visual sign of a problem. Unless you are very observant on a daily basis these signs can easily be missed. Some of the signs include lethargy, excessive scratching, muscle twitching, sudden and erratic movements for no apparent reason, lack of interest in food or water, excessive drinking, vomiting, difficulty in moving about, untypical aggression, and obvious pain, when being handled.

The most difficult problem to identify is stress. Two individuals may react totally different to certain conditions, one becoming badly stressed, another being unaffected. Stress is a subconscious negative reaction to given conditions or situations. It affects the nervous system and is a major precursor of secondary problems. It greatly diminishes the performance of the immune system. Whilst stress is difficult to diagnose, the conditions and situations likely to induce it are well known.

Lack of space, unclean conditions, excessive disturbance, rapidly changing heat levels, and proximity to something feared (which could be certain noises, or sudden changes in lighting levels, as when lights are switched on and off) can all serve as platforms to stressful behavior. It may also stem from an inadequate diet, bullying by a cage companion, or boredom.

This lilac female gerbil exhibits every outward sign of good health: alert, bright-eyed, and nicely furred.

The effect of stress can show itself in anomalous behavior. Examples would be cage bar biting, self mutilation, eating fecal matter, pacing at the cage bars, excessive eating or drinking, changing levels of aggression, cannibalism, and abandonment of young. Each of these could have an alternative cause, but should be considered as indicative of stress as well. The remedy is to ensure none of them are applicable to your pets.

REACT QUICKLY

Gerbils have a rapid metabolism. This means they can succumb to an illness very quickly — but can also recover in a likewise manner if treated promptly. Never delay in reacting once you suspect something is amiss. Remove the individual to a hospital cage where the temperature is warmer. Alternatively, leave the pet in its cage and move the entire cage to a warmer location.

Sometimes the trauma associated with taking a pet from its familiar home may stress it: this will not help matters. The seriousness of the signs will dictate which is the best course of action — the very ill gerbil is best placed in a hospital cage. Maintain water and dry food supplies, but withhold soft (moist) foods pending advice from your vet. Next, you should gather some recent fecal droppings and place these into a small plastic tub or similar. They may be required for

Good hygiene is important for your pet. Clean toys and all other cage accessories regularly.

microscopy by your vet. Make a note of the reasons you suspect the pet is unwell, and how rapidly things have deteriorated, if this has been the case.

Minor conditions, such as tummy upsets and chills, should correct themselves within twenty-four hours under warm conditions. If things get worse do not delay — consult your vet. You should, in such instances, carefully monitor the rest of your

identify given pathogens.

Treatments without diagnosis may be counterproductive. Furthermore, many antibiotics can be very dangerous to rodents. They may be non-selective on the bacteria they kill. Some bacteria are beneficial and essential in the gut of rodents to create vitamins and to help in the digestive process. Dosage of treatment is therefore critical in such small animals. Only your vet can

The more familiar you are with you gerbil's behavior, the better you will be able to discern when it is not feeling well.

stock. They may be incubating the problem as well.

DIAGNOSIS AND TREATMENTS

Do not attempt home diagnosis of gerbil illnesses. This can be fatal if you are incorrect. Many diseases display similar physical signs — how are you to know which is the one your pet has? Microscopy of fecal and blood samples is invariably needed to

determine these.

It is true that the veterinary cost of treating an ill gerbil may well be greater than the value of the pet. You must mitigate this on two accounts. Firstly, you have a moral obligation as the owner to ensure any pet is given every opportunity to lead a healthy life. Secondly, in establishing the problem you may be able to prevent other pets in your home

Four-week-old agouti Canadian white spot. As is true of the young of many species, young gerbils are very active and will spend hours exploring and playing.

Hard foods such as nuts will help to keep your gerbil's teeth at the proper length.

from contracting this. In the case of a breeder, it might make the difference between saving or losing the stock resulting from many years of carefully planned breeding.

MINOR TREATMENTS

There are some conditions that you can treat at home. Small cuts or fight wounds should be carefully bathed and smeared with a topical antiseptic or lotion. This will prevent secondary

meaning if other drugs are used at the same time these may contain similar chemicals that could prove toxic when used together.

Many treatments have a broad spectrum of use, others are target (species) specific — these would have little value if the target parasite is not identified correctly.

POSTMORTEM

Breeders who experience the sudden death of one or more of

When feeding fresh foods such as fruits and vegetables, be sure to thoroughly wash them first to remove any traces of pesticides.

infection that could be far more serious. Mites, lice and other skin and internal parasites (worms) can be treated with modern drugs. These drugs should be obtained from your vet rather than other sources that are untrained in the potential negative aspects of the drugs. Incorrect use of many modern drugs, some of which are unsuitable for gerbils, can be very dangerous. Some are unsuitable for young gerbils, some are effective at low dose rates, dangerous at high levels; others may be additive in effect,

their stock, and especially where no physical signs are apparent, are recommended to have their vet conduct a postmortem to try and establish the problem. This is not always possible, but when it is, it could prevent a major disease sweeping through a stud. Once any disease of note has been identified in your stock, it is wise to conduct an immediate full scale cleaning operation. At the same time, do review your husbandry practices to minimize the potential for history to repeat itself. Learn from problems, rather than repeat them.

EXOTIC GERBILS

This final chapter is devoted to a brief overview of a number of other gerbils and jirds that are presently regarded as exotic pets. They range from small to large. Obtaining examples will vary depending on the species. Some will be much easier to locate than others. Their housing, care, and feeding are much the same as for the popular Mongolian gerbil. Differences will be largely in respect of their size — large species will need much larger housing, and will eat more. Breeding facts and unusual features are given.

The interest in exotic pocket pets has become a market in itself these days. The higher prices for surplus bred stock means that these other gerbils and jirds will have appeal to many enthusiasts who like this small group of rodents. Because they are classified as exotic pocket pets, you must check whether they can legally be kept in your state and area. To obtain individuals you may have to look beyond your local pet store to find specialist animal dealers or importers. But start with your pet store who will probably have contact with such people.

A pair of Argente gerbils. *Meriones unguiculatus* is the scientific name given to the domestic pet gerbil.

Male gerbils: black, albino, and agouti. Male gerbils tend to be more aggressive to members of their own gender than are female gerbils.

PYGMY GERBILS

There are about forty-two species of these small gerbils found in the genera *Gerbillus* (38 species) and *Gerbillurus* (4 species). Most are of African distribution, with a few from the Middle East and two from Asia. They range in size from 11.5-33cm (4.5-13in), over half of this length comprising the tail. Their legs, especially the rear, are much longer than in the Mongolian gerbil, enabling them to make much longer leaps. The eyes appear larger by comparison to the Mongolian.

Color patterns range from a dull yellow to a bright red to gray, flecked with dark tips. Ears are larger than in the popular gerbil. The general appearance is of a more slender animal. The soles of the feet may be naked or hairy depending on the species. The pygmy gerbils are essentially nocturnal. Their habitat ranges from very dry desert to moist well cultivated areas. Like other gerbils and jirds, they live in burrows of varying sizes and complexity depending on the species. Gestation period is 20-22 days, litter size 1-8, four or five being typical.

A captive Northern Pygmy Gerbil (*Gerbillus pyramidium*) is recorded as having lived for just over eight years — a goodly lifespan for such a small rodent.

Tatra indica are known to cannibalize their litters, but this may be due to stress created by insufficient housing space.

Gestation period in *Tatera* is 24-30 days, litter size 1-13, 3-6 being typical. The young are usually independent by one month old and fully mature by four months of age. In *Taterillus* gestation is about 21 days with a litter size of 3-5. Maturity is reached when about four months old. The smaller species would make interesting subjects. The larger ones are best left to those who can provide very spacious accommodation.

SHORT-EARED GERBIL

This is quite an unusual gerbil. It is scientifically called *Desmodillus auricularis* and is the only member of its genus. It is native to Nambia, Botswana and South Africa. Unlike most gerbils, it is not especially adapted for jumping. Neither is it very social with its own kind, being more comparable to a hamster in this matter. It is about 19cm (7.5in) long, the tail taking up about 8cm (3in) of its length. The ears are very short and have a white area of fur behind them. The color pattern is orange to a tawny brown, the underbody being white. The eyes are large and round — indicative of a nocturnal species. The soles of the hind feet are hairy.

Like hamsters, this gerbil will store food in its nestbox. The sexes come together only for mating. If left together for any length of time, the female will likely kill the male. Neither are the females safe with each other, so this is very much a solitary animal—a good candidate for a little rodent pet. Gestation period is said to be twenty-one days, litter size 1-7, two to four being typical. The young are slow to mature compared with most gerbils, taking up to five weeks before they are weaned.

A similar looking gerbil is *Desmodilliscus braueri*, but this monotypic species is smaller, being on average 8cm (3in) of which the tail accounts for about one quarter. It is the smallest gerbil species and is native to Senegal, Nigeria and Sudan.

FAT-TAILED GERBIL

This interesting species, *Pachyuromys duprasi* is monotypic (meaning the only member of its genus). It is sometimes known as the Duprasi. It is native to the Sahara desert regions of Morocco and Egypt. An average length is 17cm (6.7in), of which the tail accounts for 5cm (2in).

This species is stockily built with a soft fur that may be more dense than in most gerbils. It lives in sandy sparsely vegetated areas. It is said to be very insectivorous in its dietary needs. Color pattern ranges from light yellow to a buff brown with the underbody parts white. There is a white spot area behind the ears. A characteristic feature is the short club shaped thick tail.

Gestation period is 19-22 days, litter size 3-6. Longevity is recorded at 4 $^1/_2$ years.

In the wild, most species of gerbils are nocturnal: they are active mainly at night.

BUSHY-TAILED JIRD

Looking similar to the popular gerbil, this monotypic species, *Sekeetamys calurus,* is native to Egypt, Israel, Jordan and Saudi Arabia. It is a very attractive little jird with a long bushy tipped tail, from which its scientific name is derived (*calurus*—beautiful tailed). Its size is about 23cm (9in) of which just over half is the tail. Color pattern ranges from yellow to orange red flecked with black on the back and flanks, becoming whitish on the underbody. The tail tip is often white. The soles of the hind feet are naked, the legs elongated but not excessively so.

Gestation is thought to be about 22-26 days: the average litter size is only 3 within a known range of 1-6. Recorded longevity is about 5 1/2 years.

GREAT GERBIL

For those who would like a large gerbil the monotypic species *Rhombomys opimus* should be the answer. Native to Mongolia, Afghanistan, Pakistan and former Soviet Asian territories, it has a length of about 31cm (12in). The tail accounts for just under half this length. Unlike most gerbils, this species is largely diurnal (active during daylight hours). Gestation period is 23-32 days, litter size range 1-14, half the upper number being typical. Longevity is short for gerbils — about four years for females: somewhat less for males. The great gerbil is social by nature; a number of them can be kept together if very spacious accommodation is available.

You will not find pet books specifically written on these exotic species at this time (1996). Additional information can be obtained from natural history books devoted to rodents. Field guides to the mammals of given distribution areas will also prove informative.

The pallid gerbil is also known as the Egyptian gerbil. This species is noticeably smaller than the domestic pet gerbil.

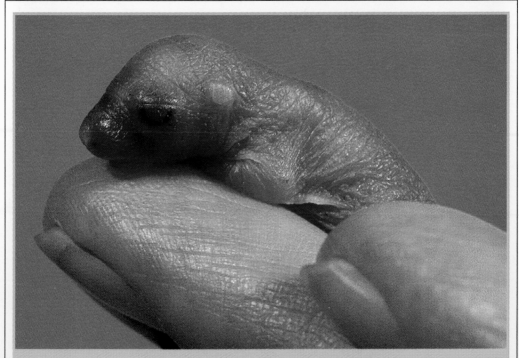

**This pallid gerbil baby is only a few hours old.
There are a little over 40 species of gerbils in the wild.**

**For Mongolian gerbils, a life span of three years is typical,
but some members of the species attain five or so years.**

GERBILS AT A GLANCE

Common Name: Gerbil or Jird

Number of Species: There are about 89 species.

Scientific Name: This is species variable. The most popular gerbils are in the genus *Meriones*, with *M.unguiculatus* (Mongolian gerbil) being the species around which the gerbil hobby developed.

Order: Rodentia. This is the largest mammalian order with over 1,800 members. Gerbils and jirds are found in the family *Gerbillinae.*

Distribution: Africa, the Middle East and Asia.

Varieties: There is a wide range of colors and patterns.

Longevity: Three years would be typical, but may attain five. In the more exotic species this can reach over eight years.

Compatibility: Very social if in family colonies. Sexes should be kept separately if continual breeding is to be avoided.

Diet: Herbivorous - Seeds, fruit, vegetables and their byproducts. Some animal origin proteins are desirable

Best Purchase Age: When over four weeks old

Breeding: Gerbils can breed when eight weeks or older. The litter size is typically 4-7. Gestation period is normally about twenty-five days. The young are weaned when 20-30 days old.

Anatomical Features: There are four digits on front feet, five on the rear. Gerbils typically have sixteen teeth of which the incisors are used for gnawing. Tail is about the same length as the body.

Desired Temperature: 61-76°F (16-24°C) is a safe range. Avoid lower or higher temperatures, and those which fluctuate rapidly within twenty-four hours.

Relative Humidity: 40-50% is probably best for most species.

Dove and agouti gerbils. Gerbils are interesting little animals that have a lot to offer as pets.